YOUR GREATEST POWER

Thirty minutes reading this inspirational classic can set off a dynamic change in your life—the very first day!

J. MARTIN KOHE

Published by:
    The Napoleon Hill Foundation
    P. O. Box 1277
    Wise, Virginia 24293

    Website: www.naphill.org
    email: napoleonhill@uvawise.edu

Distributed by:
    Executive Books
    206 W. Allen Street
    Mechanicsburg, PA 17055

    Telephone: 800-233-2665
    Website: www.executivebooks.com

ISBN Number: 0-937539-04-X

YOUR RIGHT TO CHOOSE
An Introduction By Don M. Green

We all have choices to make on a daily basis, and the sum total of these choices defines our station in life. Our choices determine if we are a part of society's ills or an instrument in the solutions that will help make the world a better place in which to live.

J. Martin Kohe, the author of *Your Greatest Power,* reveals the secret that will help you find peace of mind, happiness, good health and success.

Millions of lives have been improved by the reading and application of inspirational self-help books. Kohe distributed *Think and Grow Rich* and *Law of Success* in an effort to obtain knowledge that would help him and others become better persons and lead successful lives. More knowledge for self improvement is revealed in this great book.

Don't let the small size of this book fool you.

Your Greatest Power is a valuable motivational book for those willing to read, study and apply the message. The choice is yours.

Your Greatest Power is an easy-to-read book that can help prepare you for a better life—a life that most people dream about but never realize.

DON M. GREEN
Executive Director
The Napoleon Hill Foundation

YOUR GREATEST POWER
DISCOVERING IT

You are the possessor of a great and wonderful power. This power, when properly applied, will bring confidence instead of timidity, calmness instead of confusion, poise instead of restlessness, and peace of mind in place of a heartache.

Millions of people are complaining about their lot, disgusted with life . . . and the way things are going, not realizing that there is a power which they possess which will permit them to take a new lease on life. Once you recognize this power and begin to use it, you can change your entire life and make it the way you would like to have it. A life that was filled with sorrow can be a life filled with joy. Failure can be turned into success. Where poverty once gripped an individual's life, it can be changed to prosperity. Timidity can be turned into confidence. A life of disappointment can become a life of interesting experiences and pleasant associations. Fear can be changed to freedom.

Too many times, as life goes on, a person may have a number of reverses, he may have run into a series of difficulties, he may even have had a number of various troubles to contend with. Before long he adopts the attitude that life is difficult, that life is a battle, that the cards are stacked against him . . . so what's the use . . . "you can't win." Then this same individual settles back and is convinced that no matter what you do is "no good." Beaten in his own desire to win in life, he finally turns to his children, hoping that with them it will be different. Sometimes, this is a way out, and sometimes the children fall into the same way of life as the parent. Many times the individual comes to the conclusion that there is only one way out, and he finally comes to the end of life through his own hand . . . suicide.

Yet, all this time, the individual fails to discover this great power that will change his life. He doesn't recognize it . . . he doesn't even know it exists . . . he sees millions of others struggling the way he is and decides that THIS IS LIFE.

Raimundo DeOvies tells a story that, when the

great library of Alexandria was burned, one book was saved. But it was not a valuable book; and so a poor man, who could read a little, bought it for a few coppers. It was not very interesting; yet there was a most interesting thing in it! It was a thin strip of vellum on which was written the secret of the "Touchstone."

The touchstone was a small pebble that could turn any common metal into pure gold. The writing explained that it was on the shores of the Black Sea, lying among thousands and thousands of other pebbles which looked exactly like it. But the secret was this. The real stone would feel warm, while ordinary pebbles are cold. So the man sold his few belongings, bought some simple supplies, camped on the seashore, and began testing pebbles. This was his plan.

He knew that if he picked up ordinary pebbles and threw them down again because they were cold, he might pick up the same pebble hundreds of times. So, when he felt one that was cold, he threw it into the sea. He spent a whole day doing this and there were none of them the touchstone. Then he spent a week, a month, a year, three years; but he did not find the touchstone. Yet he went on and on this way. Pick up a pebble. It's cold. Throw it into the sea.

And so on and on.

But one morning he picked up a pebble and it was *warm* . . . he threw it into the sea. He had formed the "habit" of throwing them into the sea. He had gotten so into the habit of throwing them into the sea, that when the ONE HE WANTED CAME ALONG . . . HE STILL THREW IT AWAY.

Oh! How many times have we contacted this GREAT POWER and did not recognize it? How many times have we had THIS GREAT POWER right in our hands and we threw it away, because we did not recognize it? How often have we seen it before our very eyes? How many times have we seen THIS GREAT POWER demonstrated right before us? Yet, we did not see it with all its possibilities, with all its wonder-working effects. That is the reason we have devoted this entire treatise to THIS GREAT POWER . . . THE GREATEST POWER THAT MAN POSSESSES!

Conwell, in his book, "Acres of Diamonds," tells about a farmer who was a very happy farmer. His farm was all paid off. He had a very lovely family. Each year he managed to save some money from his plantings. He wasn't short of anything to make his life worthwhile and happy. However, one day a traveler came along and said to the farmer, "If you will find a place where water runs over white sand, there you will find diamonds. Your daughter will be richer than any princess, your son will be richer than any prince, and you will have all the wealth that you could possibly imagine." That night this farmer did not sleep . . . for the first time in many months. He rolled and tossed and turned. Finally when dawn broke he decided he would sell his farm and go out and search for diamonds. This he did. He put his family in with one of the neighbors, took his money and went all over the world searching for diamonds. Finally, when he came down to his last few cents, thoroughly disgusted with himself and what he had done, he committed suicide. In the meantime, the traveler returned to the farm. He walked into the house, looked up on the mantelpiece, and exclaimed, "Did the original owner of the farm return?" The new owner said, "No, he did not." The traveler said, "He must have, why those stones up there on the mantelpiece are diamonds." "Oh! no," exclaimed the new owner of the farm, "that's impossible . . . I found those stones out in the backyard." The traveler again assured the new owner, "Yes, those are diamonds." That is the way the Kimberley Diamond Mines in Africa were founded.

Certainly, you see the point in the story. We search all over the world looking for diamonds and still, there they are right in our own back yards. We search all through our lives for THAT POWER which will make our lives complete, but most people never find it. Yet, it is right before us. All we have to do is recognize it and start to use it. It's here.

Before we tell you what this GREAT POWER is, we want you to know about another story that took place in Africa. There was an explorer who went into the wilds of Africa. He took a number of trinkets along with him for the natives. Among some of the things that he took with him were two full-size mirrors. He placed these two mirrors against two different trees, and then sat down to talk to some of his men about the exploration. Then the explorer noticed that a savage approached the mirror with a spear in his hand. As he looked into the mirror, he saw his reflection. He began to jab his opponent in the mirror as though it were a real savage, going through all the motions of killing him. Of course, he broke the mirror into bits. In the meantime, the explorer walked over to the savage and asked him why he smashed the mirror. The native replied, "He go kill me. I kill him first." The explorer explained to the savage that that was not the purpose of the mirror, and then led the savage over to the second mirror. He explained to him. "Look, the mirror is an object whereby you may see if your hair is combed straight, to see if the paint on your face is proper, to see how chesty you are, and see how muscular you are." The savage replied, "Oh! me no know."

So it is with so many millions of people. They go through life fighting it. They expect a battle at every turn and that is the way it turns out. They expect to have enemies, and they certainly do. They expect to have one difficulty after another, and that is exactly the way it happens. "If it isn't one thing, it's another . . . there is always something" . . . and that is the way it has been and will continue to be for millions of people who fail to recognize this GREAT POWER. This GREAT POWER that could completely change the world remains as hidden as the diamonds from the farmer who had them in his own back yard. Millions of people will continue to live plain, ordinary, miserable lives because this GREAT POWER escapes them and they never have been able to catch up with it. YOU CAN'T FIGHT LIFE. You have tried it. Millions have tried it and have failed. Then what is the answer? THE ANSWER IS THAT WE MUST UNDERSTAND

LIFE . . . IF WE WISH TO MAKE THE MOST OF IT.

The amazing part about this power is that anyone and everyone can use it. It doesn't require any special training or education. It isn't a power that requires any special aptitudes to make it work successfully. It isn't a power that anyone has any special claims to, nor does it require wealth or prestige to make it work. It is a power that everyone is given at birth, whether he be rich or poor, successful or unsuccessful, whether he be born on the right side of the tracks or not. The sooner we recognize this power, the quicker we get on the main road and stay there. The more of us who will get on the main road and stay there, the more hope will spring in the hearts of others to follow this healthy pattern of life.

Millions of people fail to realize that when they go into a shoe store, they may choose to buy a pair of black shoes or they may choose to buy a pair of brown shoes; that when they go into a clothing store, they choose to buy a light garment or they choose to buy a dark garment; that when they turn on the radio, they may choose to tune in one station or they may choose to tune in another station; that when they go into an ice cream parlor, they may choose to buy a chocolate sundae or a pineapple soda; that when they go to the movies, they may choose to go to a neighborhood movie or they may choose to go to a downtown movie. Yes, it is true, if you CHOOSE, when you go on a vacation, to go to the seashore instead of going to the mountains, that YOU MADE THIS CHOICE. When you buy a car YOU CHOOSE to buy a car of one particular make or YOU CHOOSE to buy a car of another manufacturer. In other words, THE GREATEST POWER THAT A PERSON POSSESSES IS . . .

THE POWER TO CHOOSE.

Yes, you have this power, regardless of your religious beliefs. You choose the shoes, the car, the radio program, the picture show, the vacation, the mate. You have this power. There was nothing outside of yourself to force you to make the decision that you did. You did it, because you made this choice. You made this choice because YOU WANTED IT SO. If the choice was bad, then, of course, we want something or someone to blame. So, some people will say, "It was God's Will." But was it? You are probably familiar with the old saying "God helps those that help themselves." Regardless of what we believe regarding God, God does give each and every man and woman the right TO HELP HIMSELF . . . OR IN OTHER WORDS,

THE RIGHT TO CHOOSE.

Henry Drummond in his book "The Greatest Thing in the World" tells a story of a little boy who was very sick. The boy was going to die. The parents were very much upset about it, and yet, there was nothing the doctors could do. One day an elderly, religious man walked into the house and noticed how depressed everyone was. He asked why they were so downhearted. He was told that their little son was very sick and they expected the little fellow to die. The religious man asked where the boy was and he was told which bedroom to go to. The elderly religious man walked into the bedroom, put his hand on the little fellow's head and said, "My boy, GOD LOVES YOU, don't you know that?" and walked out of the room, then shortly afterward left the home. After he had gone, the little fellow who was sick and was going to die, jumped out of bed, ran all over the house shouting, "God loves me . . . GOD LOVES ME." He no longer was sick, but a well, strong and healthy boy.

Here is a perfect illustration of what happens when a person CHOOSES to believe that God loves him. No doubt, the little fellow had done something which was wrong . . . certainly not anything punishable by death . . . but he evidently thought that God was punishing him. But once he made the realization that GOD LOVED HIM, he was no longer sick. The little fellow made use of that GREAT POWER . . . THE POWER TO CHOOSE. It gave him life. It saved the family much sorrow and heartache.

Too many people have the very bad habit of telling their children that God will punish them if they do something wrong. The child is filled with fear . . . the fear of God. He chooses to be afraid of God. The child goes into adult life . . . still with this fear. Is it any wonder that the average person's life is a shadow of what real living could be? He, in turn, does the same thing with his children. And so, century after century, this fear is perpetuated by parents who fail to understand that THE POWER TO CHOOSE can change their lives. If telling the child that God will punish him would prevent the evil doing, it would be all right . . . but look around and you will see that it has not turned the trick. On the other hand, if we would realize *that the wrong doing itself carries with it its own punishment,* then we will CHOOSE what is right. Because we will then know that it isn't God that is going to punish us, but it is our own BAD CHOOSING that carries the punishment with it. If we make the right choice in the first place, what can go wrong?

For example, a woman who had a very lovely son was constantly in the habit of telling her little boy that if he did not do what was right, God would punish him. The result was that the little fellow was always having colds. The mother was beside herself; she didn't know what to do. Then she learned that you don't say that to a child. You tell a child that God loves him. She explained this to the child, with the result that the child no longer had any colds. The mother was amazed and astounded. Here you can see as long as the mother CHOSE to tell her youngster that God would punish him, he was filled with colds . . . when she CHOSE to tell her son that GOD LOVES YOU, the change came about. WHAT BROUGHT ABOUT THE CHANGE? Did God make the change? It was the mother, who in CHOOSING THE RIGHT IDEA OF PRESENTING GOD changed her child's life and her own.

We must, therefore, realize that there is NOTHING OUTSIDE OF OURSELVES to hurt us. GOD DOESN'T HURT US. GOD LOVES US. THEREFORE, WHAT CAN HURT US . . . *ONLY OUR OWN BAD CHOOSING.*

If we choose to eat so much that we make ourselves sick, who is to blame? If we choose to drive our cars so fast that we cannot control them, who is to blame? If we choose to allow ourselves to have nasty, disagreeable personalities, who is to blame? If we try to become the "richest man in the cemetery" and make ourselves invalids, who is to blame? If we have failed to learn how to live, whom shall we blame? God? Oh, no! not any more. GOD LOVES YOU. He doesn't hurt anybody. We hurt ourselves through the bad use of this GREAT POWER that God gave us . . . THE POWER TO CHOOSE.

Choosing Wealth

Millions of people are seeking wealth. They would like to be able to say to themselves, "Now, I don't have to worry about money anymore." They would love to be free from money worries. So they scheme, plan and try many different ways to help themselves financially and nothing seems to work. The result is that they become discouraged, and decide that they are not the ones who will achieve this enviable position. They tried everything but changing their thoughts—the one thing that would make the difference.

Some time ago we came in contact with a man who was having all kinds of financial trouble. His wife complained that she was afraid to go to the door, because the only people who came to the door were bill collectors. It was a very discouraging situation. We gave this family a book that we thought would help them improve their thinking. The wife looked at the book and said, "I wouldn't read that stuff . . . there is nothing to it." The husband said, "I'll read it, leave it here." The result was that the man began to think differently. He showed a new spirit for living. Within a year's time, they moved into a better neighborhood; they bought a whole houseful of new furniture; he even made a down payment on a new car.

We did not give the man any money. Certainly money would have helped him, but it would only have been a temporary lift. What we did do was to start the man on the right road of CHOOSING HIS THOUGHTS FOR IMPROVING HIS FINANCIAL STATUS. That is what we need, if we are going to improve our financial positions. If we do not change our thinking, we can never hope to change our financial positions. What most of us fail to realize is that A TOOTH GROWS FROM THE INSIDE OUT. So, we must change our inner thoughts . . . as we change our inner thoughts about our financial positions, the outward change is bound to come about. So LET US CHOOSE GOOD, HEALTHY THOUGHTS ABOUT MONEY AND FINANCES.

By using this GREAT POWER TO CHOOSE in the right direction, you are bound to improve your financial station. But too many people through their own failure to use this great power have made themselves slaves to the very thing they have wanted to avoid. There was a young man for whom life had been quite a struggle. He had been unemployed for quite a length of time. He finally obtained employment that was by no means anything to be proud of. Yet, this same young man, who was married and had a youngster, had the nerve to say, "I don't want to be rich." He was trying to set aside a few pennies every day so that his son would be able to go to college some day. This man was wise enough to choose to set aside a little money for his son's education. To say that it was a struggle is putting it mildly. He refused to go to a downtown movie, instead preferred to go to a neighborhood show, in order to save a quarter. He refused to go to a better type restaurant because it would cost more money. When he went to the legitimate theater, he would buy balcony seats, instead of orchestra, because that was all that he could afford. When he bought a car, he bought the most economical kind of car. He was unable to take his family on a vacation, because he couldn't afford to do it. This man had the nerve to choose to say, "I don't want to be rich."

Is it any wonder that millions of people are

steeped in poverty? NOT REALIZING IT, THEY CHOOSE TO REMAIN POOR. THEY FAIL TO RECOGNIZE THIS GREAT POWER. No one can be blamed for being economical. Many people must be thrifty or they would not get along at all. But these same people could be making use of this GREAT POWER TO CHOOSE. They could start to fill their minds with the better things of life.

Instead, we hear day after day people saying, "I would like that, but I can't afford it." "I can't afford it." "I can't afford it." It's true, BUT DON'T SAY IT. As long as you continue to say "I CAN'T AFFORD IT" . . . *you will go all through your life* with "I CAN'T AFFORD IT." CHOOSE A BETTER THOUGHT. Say, "I'll buy it. I'll get it." When you build up the thought that you will get it, that you will buy it, you build up the thought of expectancy. YOU BUILD UP YOUR HOPE. NEVER DESTROY YOUR HOPE. When you destroy your hope, then you have created for yourself a life of difficulty and disappointment.

A young man who didn't have a dollar to his name said, "One of these days, I am going to Europe." A friend sitting by started to laugh and said, "Look who's talking." Twenty years later the man and his wife went to Europe. The man did not say, "I want to go to Europe and I suppose I never will be able to afford it." He had the hope. The hope gave him spirit. The spirit moved him to do things so that he would be able to go to Europe. When you say "I can't afford it" . . . everything stops. The hope is gone . . . the mind becomes dulled . . . the spirit is gone . . . then WE CHOOSE to believe that nothing can be done about it. THIS GREAT POWER . . . THE POWER TO CHOOSE will give you the necessary hope, the necessary spirit, the necessary courage to carry on and GET THE THINGS FROM LIFE THAT YOU REALLY WANT.

Allen in his little book "As a Man Thinketh" says that "Thoughts are Things." We like to change it to read THOUGHTS BECOME THINGS. The telephone was a thought in the mind of Bell before it became a telephone. The harvester was a thought in the mind of McCormick before it became a harvester. The electric bulb was a thought in the mind of Edison before it became an electric bulb. John D. Rockefeller, when he didn't have a dime to his name, said, "Some day I am going to become a millionaire." AND HE DID. So you must realize that the things that you want out of life are thoughts first before they become things. Our financial condition is a thought first, and then a reality. If we want to change our financial picture, we must first CHANGE OUR THOUGHT. If we CHOOSE TO CHANGE OUR INNER THOUGHTS . . . our outer conditions must change. THAT'S THE LAW. When you choose thoughts of "I can't afford it" . . . "I'll never get it" . . . "I am one of the blessed poor" . . . you are blocking the pathway to YOUR GOOD. CHOOSE YOUR THOUGHTS . . . YOU CAN . . . CHANGE YOUR THOUGHTS . . . YOU CAN . . . use your imagination in the beginning, if necessary. You will never regret it. Things will begin to happen for you, changes will come into your life, such as you never believed possible. YOU WILL TRULY GAIN A NEW LEASE ON LIFE.

It is surprising how many times THIS GREAT POWER . . . THE POWER TO CHOOSE . . . if used correctly could make a person's life what he wants it to be. One young man had a very unusual experience. He found that every time he saved up to seventy dollars, something would happen. He would have an accident . . . some unforeseen difficulty would arise . . . HE JUST COULDN'T SAVE OVER SEVENTY DOLLARS. This man will go through life with this problem and difficulty, unless he uses this GREAT POWER . . . THE POWER TO CHOOSE and starts to think differently.

Another man found that every time he had a little money in the bank . . . something would happen so that he JUST COULDN'T KEEP IT for any length of time. He went through his whole life with this thought . . . he could have just as easily used his GREAT POWER . . . THE POWER TO CHOOSE . . . and changed this thought destroyer.

One young man was a jack-of-all-trades. He was able to do many things well. Although he was successful in everything that he did, nevertheless, he never made any money. People could not understand why. He was ambitious. He was likable. He had a pleasing personality, but financially, he struggled year after year. Finally this young man had it pointed out to him just what his trouble was. He constantly made the statement, "I can do everything well but make money." Once he began to realize that his big trouble was simply a bad choice of thought . . . things began to change. Instead of saying, "I can do everything well but make money," he began to say, "I can do everything well, including making money." Within a few years' time this man's financial condition changed. He really and truly started to make money. He began to get ahead financially, until today, people say that he is a rich man. This man could have gone through his whole life doing many things well, but never making any money. As soon as he realized that he was CHOOSING THE WRONG THOUGHT, and did something about changing that thought, then his financial condition turned for the better. THE POWER TO CHOOSE brings about a much better and effective money-making power.

CHOOSING CONDITIONS

Anyone with a little common sense knows that you cannot control conditions. Unless, of course, you happen to become the head of your government, and maybe then you would be able to control them.

But for most of us, we must agree that we cannot control conditions. This is true. So, what can we do? We can control our thoughts . . . and by controlling our thoughts . . . by USING THIS GREATEST POWER . . . THE POWER TO CHOOSE . . . we are INDIRECTLY ABLE TO CONTROL CONDITIONS. The most common illustration is in time of war. A young man is called into the service. Here he has no choice. He must go and serve his country. He is brought to camp. Here he is trained. He is prepared for action. All during this time HE HAD NO CHOICE as to what his officers made him do. He had to comply with their demands. BUT HE STILL HAD THE POWER TO CHOOSE HIS OWN THOUGHTS. If he chose the thought that he would not come out alive, that he would be crippled . . . it wouldn't be a surprise that this is exactly what happened. We know that on the other hand, that a person or soldier can protect himself through his own POWER TO CHOOSE. F. L. Rawson, noted engineer, and one of England's greatest scientists, in his book, "Life Understood," gives account of a British regiment under control of Colonel Whittlesey, which served in the World War for more than four years without losing a man. This unparalleled record was made possible by means of active cooperation of officers and men in memorizing and repeating regularly the words of the 91st Psalm which has been called the Psalm of Protection. This is an extreme case of the POWER TO CHOOSE, but remember it is the GREATEST POWER THAT MAN POSSESSES.

We all know that there are good times and bad times. Some people can't even make a living in good times, let alone in bad times, mainly because they have failed to use THIS GREATEST POWER . . . THE POWER TO CHOOSE. When bad times come along, most people sit back, fill themselves with discouragement and wait for the government to do something about it. Others will use this GREATEST POWER . . . THE POWER TO CHOOSE . . . and will make a success even in bad times. Many of our greatest businesses have been started and built in "so-called" bad times. Why? Because the founders of the business refused to believe in bad times . . . they went ahead anyway . . . and succeeded. In bad times, there are many times the number of advantages which good times do not allow. Less money is needed to start and keep the business going, help is easier to get and cheaper, competition is not so alert . . . and more than anything else, there are so many discouraged people that the PERSON WITH A LITTLE COURAGE doesn't have to battle so hard.

There was a man who was in business during one of the "bad time" periods. He felt that the reason he was not doing so well was due to the bad times. He felt that unless conditions improved, there would be no opportunity for him to improve. Then during the very heart of the bad time period, he went into a certain shopping district. He noticed that there were two butchers within 10 stores of one another. One was as busy as he could be. People were standing three and four deep to be waited on. The other butcher hardly had a customer. Here is a problem. Bad times exist. Yet within the very same neighborhood there are two butchers, one who doesn't even know there is such a thing as bad times, and the other one is barely making a living. The young business man decided to investigate. He went into the store where the people were standing waiting for service, and as he did, the store owner said, "How do you do?" in a very pleasing and courteous manner, "I am busy, but I will be with you in a few minutes." He was gentle and kind with each and every customer. He was helpful and serviceable to people. He made suggestions to his customers, but at no time argued with them. The purchase was made. Then several days later, the young business man went to the other store. The proprietor growled, "What is it you want?" Instead of giving the young man the meat he wanted, this butcher attempted to force upon him the meat the butcher thought he ought to have. He was not pleasant at all, and was interested only in his immediate welfare. Here you can quickly recognize THE POWER TO CHOOSE.

The one butcher chose to believe that business was bad, due to the bad times, and that was the way it worked out for him. He was not a courteous and reasonable person with his customers. Furthermore, he even preferred to take his "bad business" out on the very people who came in to patronize him. The other butcher chose to believe that business was up to him. It was up to him to be fair and reasonable. It was up to him to be courteous and helpful. He didn't know what bad times were. He chose correctly. The man with little to do chose incorrectly. This ability TO RECOGNIZE THIS GREATEST POWER . . . THE POWER TO CHOOSE . . . makes it possible for a person to get the most out of life, while the other person not recognizing this power makes life a burden. THE POWER TO CHOOSE helps one to increase his money-making ability.

The young business man, after noticing the difference between the two butchers, went to his office the next day and started to work. HE CHOSE TO BELIEVE IT WAS UP TO HIM . . . not to the times or the government. He started to advertise, he made special sales, he made necessary changes for the times, he modified his prices, and before long he was busy again . . . business was good again . . . he was making money again. CONDITIONS HAD NOT CHANGED. BUT HE DID. Through this GREATEST POWER . . . THE POWER TO CHOOSE . . . instead of closing his doors, his business was once more on its feet . . .

he had changed . . . even though the times had not.

In the field of employment, we have a similar situation. Let us take two employees and compare them and see how THE POWER TO CHOOSE AFFECTS EACH PERSON. One always chooses to be to work on time. He chooses to follow instructions. He chooses to do his work the very best that he knows how. He chooses to offer suggestions which may help the business. He chooses to do certain little odds and ends which may not be in his keeping with the position for which he was hired. He chooses to work a few minutes, or even an hour over-time if necessary. He chooses to study the business, even taking special courses after working hours to improve himself and the services of the company. This man, through his simple POWER TO CHOOSE, makes himself a successful employee who is bound to make progress. He makes himself so valuable to his employer, that his employer goes out of his way, if necessary, to keep this person employed.

Now let us take a look at the other kind of employee. He chooses to come to work at a time suitable to himself. He chooses to argue with his employer and his fellow-workers about certain things which have to be done. He refuses to work a few minutes or an hour overtime. He chooses to go outside of the business and talk against his company. He chooses to do only as much work as he is paid for. He chooses to spend his time in foolish entertainment and ungainly activities. He chooses to feel that the time outside of working hours belongs to him and he may do with it as he pleases. He chooses to refuse to look into the future, or to prepare himself for the future.

When bad times come around, the second man will be the first one let out. He will blame the times. He starts to complain bitterly because he lost his job. He will rant against his government, calling the heads of his government all kinds of nasty names. He will blame everybody but himself. His family and associates suffer along with him. He chooses to let the days and years go by. He finally finds himself in a home for the aged, which is kept up by the state. Why?

If there were only some way that people could be made to realize that THIS GREATEST POWER . . . THE POWER TO CHOOSE . . . and choose correctly *EXISTS WITHIN THEIR OWN MINDS,* that they could carry out the plans of their own choice and really live the way they may have dreamed of living. It is easy enough to blame conditions; it is easy enough to blame relatives; it is easy enough to blame the government; it is easy enough to blame anybody and everybody and everything, if ONE CHOOSES TO DO SO. But, any person who truly recognizes this GREATEST POWER . . . THE POWER TO CHOOSE . . . begins to make progress, not only in his business life, but also in his social, family and personal life. He begins to realize that he is the one THAT IS DOING THE CHOOSING and that friends, although they mean well, cannot do his choosing for him, nor can his relatives. Consequently, he develops real self-confidence based upon his own ability, upon his own actions, and upon his own initiative. No longer does he depend upon conditions. No longer does he depend upon some figure of imagination, but instead, he depends upon himself; the results begin to tell right from the beginning of his realization. *This realization seems so difficult because hundreds of thoughts are racing through our minds at such speed that we fail to recognize this simple yet amazing POWER TO CHOOSE.*

Choosing Your Personality

One of the greatest problems in life is the problem of personality. Personalities seem to be clashing constantly. Many of our troubles and difficulties come about because people cannot get along with one another. Homes are broken up, friendships are destroyed, employment problems by the hundreds arise because of a clash of personalities . . . and even wars are engaged in because of different nations failing to see eye to eye.

Here again, the GREATEST POWER man possesses . . . THE POWER TO CHOOSE . . . plays a most important part. Stop to think about it . . . you can choose to be friendly, or you can choose to be unfriendly. You can choose to be helpful, or you can choose to refuse to help. You can choose to be cooperative, or you can choose to be stubborn. You can choose to get excited, or you can choose to be calm. You can choose to lose your temper, or you can choose to overlook the matter which would ordinarily cause you to be upset. You can choose to be lovable, or you can choose to be bitter. You can choose to smile, or you can choose to walk around with a long face. You can choose to be trusting, or you can choose to distrust everyone you meet. You can choose to believe that "everybody is against you," or you can choose to believe that everybody likes you. You can choose to be neat and clean, or you can choose to be careless and slovenly. You can choose to be lazy, or you can choose to be ambitious. Stop to think about it AGAIN. Don't you do your own choosing? YOU CERTAINLY DO. Here is one of the best cases on record.

Benjamin Franklin came to the strange awakening that he was constantly losing friends. He began to realize that he was constantly arguing with people. HE JUST COULDN'T GET ALONG WITH PEOPLE. One day, around New Year's Day, when New Year's resolutions are generally made, he sat down and made a list of all his nasty personality characteristics. He listed them one by one. He arranged them, putting the most harmful trait at the top of the list, down to the least harmful. Then he decided that he would eliminate these

nasty personality characteristics one by one. Each
time that he found that he had successfully elimi-
nated one, he would cross it off the list, until he had
cleaned up the entire list. He developed one of the
finest personalities in America. Everybody looked
up to him and admired him. When the colonies
needed help from France, they sent Franklin. The
French liked Franklin so well that they gave him
what he asked for. TODAY IN ALMOST ALL
YOUR BOOKS ON PERSONALITY BUILDING,
THE NAME OF BENJAMIN FRANKLIN is cited as
the most outstanding case of personality develop-
ment.

Suppose on the other hand, Franklin had
CHOSEN to go through life without doing anything
about his personality. Suppose Franklin had done
what millions of people are doing today . . . using
their personalities just as it was given to them by
nature and their parents. Suppose that Franklin
continued his argumentative ways . . . he never would
have succeeded in getting the French to help the
colonies, and the entire history of the United States
would have been changed. ONE PERSONALITY
made a great difference to a nation. And yet, millions
of people are walking around and saying, "What can
I do about it?" How do you know? How do you

know what YOU might be able to do as the years go by. Lincoln said, "I will prepare myself and some day my time will come." AND IT DID. HE CHOSE TO BELIEVE in preparedness. AT LEAST WE WILL MAKE LIFE REASONABLE AND ENJOYABLE FOR THOSE AROUND US. AT LEAST WE WILL NOT BE RESPONSIBLE FOR BRINGING UNNECESSARY TROUBLE TO THOSE ABOUT US.

How many times does one member of a family make life miserable for everybody else in the family? How often does an unreasonable father or maybe even a mother make all the other members of the family wish that they had never been born into that family. One person can destroy or make an entire family miserable. YET, THIS SAME PERSON, BY USING THE GREATEST POWER GIVEN TO MAN . . . THE POWER TO CHOOSE . . . COULD HAVE MADE A BEAUTIFUL LIFE FOR THOSE AROUND HIM AND ESPECIALLY THE MEMBERS OF HIS OWN IMMEDIATE FAMILY. If each one of us would make his own family life a pleasant and enjoyable experience, THE WHOLE WORLD COULD BE CHANGED IN A VERY SHORT TIME.

One problem that faces many people as they go

through life is the loss of a beloved one. So many people, after losing a mother, father, brother, or a close friend or relative, become so upset that life to them becomes meaningless. "What is there to live for now?" they ask. All over the world there are thousands upon thousands of people who walk through the streets and through the balance of their lives "living corpses." Failing to realize that they possess this GREATEST POWER . . . THE POWER TO CHOOSE . . . they continue their lives choosing to be a burden to themselves and everyone around them. You cannot blame these people, for their loss was great. The shock may have been very sudden, for apparently no reason. They are unable to analyze why it had to happen. Sometimes it is not easy to analyze why it happened. But whether we can analyze it or not, the important job on hand now is what to do with the balance of life that remains to the one left behind.

We feel that the best way to answer this great question is through a story that we came across some time ago. A young college football star lost his mother the week before the "big game." The coach didn't know what to do. He had never had an experience like this before. He finally decided that he would leave it up to the young star himself.

If the boy decided to play, that would be fine with the coach. However, if the young man decided that the shock was too great and that he would decide not to play, then the coach would abide by his decision. The day of the game came. The team ran out on the field. The young star was with them. The team proceeded to go through with their practice signals, while the young football star went over to the stands. He stood there. About twelve rows up in the stand there was an empty seat. It was draped in black. The young man stood there . . . looked at the empty seat draped in black and said, "Mother, I am playing this game for you." He then went into the game and helped his team to victory.

Here is a splendid illustration of the POWER TO CHOOSE. This young man could have sat down and started to cry. He could have made himself the subject of sympathy from all his fellow teammates. He could have made them all feel so sorry that the entire team would have been affected and the game would have been lost. But he chose for the benefit of all. He benefited, his team benefited, and surely, his mother wherever she was, was really proud of her son. He was playing the WAY SHE WOULD HAVE WANTED HIM TO. That is the answer. After the beloved one has passed on,

what can we do about it? Go on living THE WAY
THEY WOULD WANT US TO LIVE.   MAKE
THEM PROUD OF US WHEREVER THEY ARE.
True, we cannot control conditions . . . but we can
control our POWER TO CHOOSE. In controlling
our POWER TO CHOOSE, we can make life interesting and worthwhile to ourselves and everyone else
around us.

   We look at all the problems of life and they
seem insurmountable. We look around and we
wonder if life will ever be worthwhile. Some people
will go so far as to say that the world is getting worse
instead of better. The world will start getting better
the very minute WE CHOOSE TO MAKE IT
BETTER. Do not wait for the other fellow to start
improving the world. Do not wait for your neighbor
to start improving himself . . . YOU START. If each
one of us will start to CHOOSE TO IMPROVE
HIMSELF, WE CAN CHANGE OUR OWN
LITTLE WORLDS, THE LITTLE WORLD THAT
EACH AND EVERYONE OF US LIVE IN. THAT'S
THE MOST IMPORTANT ONE FOR US. *THAT
IS THE ONE WE CAN DO SOMETHING ABOUT.*
Each one of us may have five or a hundred and five
people that we can come in contact with. If we have
a pleasant and helpful influence on these five or one

hundred and five, our influence on them will be for the better . . . they in turn will influence others in a similar manner . . . it won't take as long as you might think to change this world to be a BETTER PLACE TO LIVE IN.

Some time ago we saw an article in the paper about a certain street that was to be made into a boulevard by the governmental authorities. The plans were all made and everybody sat back and waited for the powers that be to start to make the necessary improvements. It was going to be a "million dollar boulevard." But something happened. The government officials found it impossible to go ahead with the plans and the idea was tabled. One man who lived on the boulevard CHOSE TO DO SOMETHING ABOUT IT. He decided that if the government officials were not going to beautify the boulevard, the least he could do was to beautify his own front yard. This he did. It was one of the most attractive places on the boulevard. His neighbor saw what he did and the neighbor began to beautify his place; this continued with each neighbor, until the entire boulevard looked like the "million dollar boulevard." WHO DID IT? Actually, ONE MAN. HE CHOSE TO START AND EVERYBODY ELSE FOLLOWED.

Don't say that you can't change the world. YOU CAN CHANGE YOUR LITTLE WORLD . . . and that's the one that counts. YOU CHOOSE TO THINK THAT YOU CAN CHANGE IT . . . THE NEXT FELLOW WILL GET THE IDEA AND IT WILL BE DONE . . . AND YOU CAN BE THE VERY PERSON TO START IT IN YOUR OWN HOME, JOB, COMMUNITY, OR EVEN IN YOUR COUNTRY.

Practically every personality problem could be solved if we would ONLY CHOOSE TO FOLLOW one simple little suggestion. So many husbands and wives are living miserable family lives because of various disagreements. Millions of people working on jobs are having their hands full because of many different forms of disagreements. Even nations find themselves at war because of unsettled disagreements. If these people involved would use this GREATEST POWER GIVEN TO MAN . . . THE POWER TO CHOOSE . . . we would find ourselves in an altogether different style of living. Many, many years ago a wise old philosopher said,

"IF WE MUST DISAGREE . . .
LET US DISAGREE WITHOUT
BEING DISAGREEABLE."

If we would realize as individuals, if we would

realize as husbands and wives, that two people living together are bound to have differences of opinion . . . that it is perfectly alright to disagree . . . BUT WITHOUT BEING DISAGREEABLE . . . THE ENTIRE NATIONAL PICTURE OF MARRIAGE WOULD CHANGE OVERNIGHT. Marriage could be so much more enjoyable. Home life could be so much more worthwhile. The influence on the children would be tremendous. The divorce rate would be cut so deeply, it would be unbelievable.

The great difference of opinion in the minds of employees is such that millions of people are unhappy in their work. Many times, these people find that they like the work, they like the pay, they enjoy the surroundings, but THEY CANNOT GET ALONG WITH CERTAIN PEOPLE. Thousands are constantly changing jobs, because of differences of opinions. If these people would use this GREATEST POWER . . . THE POWER TO CHOOSE . . . and disagree without being disagreeable . . . they would find themselves much happier, much more enjoyably engaged in their work, and much freer and easier with the people they come in contact with. It would be a great burden off their shoulders, because instead of fighting people and conditions, they would be more alerted to understanding others and their opinions.

Most of us have had the experience of going through one or two wars or even more. We have observed that it is one thing to win a war and another thing to win the peace. It is most interesting when you think about it, that the very nation you defeat in war, you must, after the war, feed and clothe, help the conquered nation to its feet again, give her financial aid so that her economy will be self-sustaining. To what end? One never knows. To start another conflict? To recreate the very thing you sought to destroy? Will the nations of the world some day use this GREATEST POWER . . . THE POWER TO CHOOSE . . . and save themselves these great catastrophes? Will the nations of the world some day CHOOSE TO DISAGREE WITHOUT BEING DISAGREEABLE? Let us hope they will. THEY CAN. Just as we can use this GREATEST POWER . . . THE POWER TO CHOOSE . . . to make our own individual lives worthwhile and enjoyable; just as we can use this POWER TO CHOOSE to make our family lives agreeable and happy, so can the nations of the world make the family of nations, one GREAT BIG HAPPY FAMILY. Sounds too wonderful? WE HAVE THE POWER . . . WE CAN, IF WE CHOOSE TO.

How can one be so sure? Go to a symphony

sometime, or watch a great symphony orchestra on the television. What do you see? A hundred men or more playing one great musical selection. Notice a little more and you will see many, many different kinds of instruments, each making its own sound and contributing its own bit to the entire musical selection. Different instruments, yes . . . but disagreeing . . . not at all. Each player plays for the good of all. No conflicts . . . all in harmony. Each player desires to make the selection the most brilliant piece of music ever played. Each man gains pleasure in making this great production possible. Each man's pride swells as he notices the great musical selection draw to its close.

Analyze this great symphonic orchestra a little closer and what do you find. Each man chose to play in the orchestra. Each man chose to play the particular instrument that he was using. Each man chose to harmonize with the other players. Each man chose to do the best that he knew how. He chose to follow the conductor, as he directed them through the selection.

SO CAN WE. We have been given this power. We have been given this GREATEST POWER . . . THE POWER TO CHOOSE . . . by the GREAT CONDUCTOR. THE GREAT CONDUCTOR

LOVES US. THE GREAT CONDUCTOR WANTS US TO GET ALONG. YES, WE ARE ALL DIFFERENT. Different customs, different foods, different mannerisms, different languages, but not so different that we cannot get along with each other . . . IF WE WILL DISAGREE WITHOUT BEING DISAGREEABLE. THE GREAT CONDUCTOR has often been referred to as OUR FATHER. Being OUR FATHER, he has made it possible to live together as one great peaceful family. He has made it possible, by giving US THE POWER TO CHOOSE. WILL WE USE IT SENSIBLY OR WILL WE USE IT FOOLISHLY? WE HAVE THE POWER . . . THIS GREATEST POWER . . . THE POWER TO CHOOSE.

Choosing Happiness

Almost everyone could find himself 100 to 500 percent happier, if he could recognize and realize that he possesses THIS GREATEST POWER . . . THE POWER TO CHOOSE . . . So many people have a little happiness and then try to hang on to it. Some people as soon as they find themselves a little happy, wonder what is wrong and especially begin to wonder if it will last. There was a play on Broadway in which the heroine walks out on the stage (she had just returned from her honeymoon) and states she is so happy "she could die." Just imagine . . . here is a person who was searching for happiness . . . now that she has it "she could die." What a terrible MISUSE of the GREATEST POWER . . . THE POWER TO CHOOSE. Is it any wonder that we see so little happiness? Those who have it are so afraid that they cannot hold on to it, that they lose it almost as fast as they find it.

Sometime ago a young man told us this story. He said, "I was going with a young lady. We became very fond of each other. We decided to become engaged. So happy were we in our engagement that we decided to culminate our happiness in marriage. We were married. We fixed up a very attractive little apartment. In fact, it was the envy of all our friends. My wife was working. I was working. We had a car. We had a little money in the bank. We were really and truly living a heaven on earth. But, from time to time, I would talk with some of my friends, and they seemed to feel that it wouldn't last. They told me that it couldn't last. They would say, 'Look at the Joneses, how happy they were the first few months of their married life. Look at them now, how much trouble and worry they have. Look at the Smiths. They were happy, too, the first few months of their married life. Look how unhappy they are now.' I heard this so many times that I thought that my wife and I were living an unnatural life instead of a natural one, that any day this heaven-on-earth marriage balloon would burst. I would go home, after talking to one of these people who said it was too good to last, and say the same thing to my wife. 'Dear, this is too good to last. It is too heavenly. It just can't go on.' Before long, things began to happen. My wife lost her job. I lost my job. We had to give up our car. We had to give up our beautiful little apartment that we had fixed up. We had to go back and live with mother, and on top of it all, my wife became a mother herself. What's the good of living," he cried out, "if every time you get things straightened out, something comes along to spoil it." He wanted to commit suicide. He felt that if THIS IS LIFE, then you might as well end it now.

We finally showed the young man that had he used his GREATEST POWER . . . THE POWER TO CHOOSE . . . HE COULD HAVE AVOIDED ALL OF THIS DIFFICULTY. We showed him that he did not have to CHOOSE TO BELIEVE his friends who told him that married happiness does not and cannot last. We told him about a wonderful statement that a woman wrote in her book that would have saved him all this difficulty. Florence Scovell Shinn, author of the "Game of Life and How to Play It" and also, "Your Word Is Your Wand" states in the latter book that *NOTHING IS TOO GOOD TO LAST.* We explained to him that there isn't anything that will come along to spoil your life, if you use your POWER TO CHOOSE CORRECTLY. If you use your POWER TO CHOOSE that NOTHING IS TOO GOOD TO LAST, it is surprising but true, that things will run along smoothly and beautifully for you, even beyond your fondest dreams. *HERE IS THE SECRET OF KEEPING THINGS RUNNING SMOOTHLY.* But, you must constantly remind yourself that when everything is going without trouble that THAT IS THE WAY IT IS SUPPOSED TO BE. The stars don't bump into the moon; the moon does not crash into the sun; the sun does not crash into the earth. Certainly, if the stars and the moon and the earth, traveling at a tremendous pace don't conflict with one another, why can't our lives run along smoothly without the conflicting forces that so many people encounter. Our lives can run along without friction, if we could only realize the full import of the POWER TO CHOOSE. THE POWER TO CHOOSE THAT NOTHING IS TOO GOOD TO LAST will make a change in your life far greater than one could even dream of. As one man said, "Our heaven on earth is right here, but the trouble with most of us is that we don't take advantage of it."

Everywhere you go you hear of people who are getting along beautifully, and then seem to have trouble holding on to this smooth living. A man is getting along exceptionally well in his work. He is happily married. He has money in the bank. He drives a big car. He is sitting on "top of the world." But can he stand it? No! He doesn't see anyone else living so smoothly. He thinks he is better than the next fellow. He becomes overconfident. Overconfidence always leads to carelessness. This carelessness leads him into trouble of one form or another. NOW HE IS DISCOURAGED. Didn't he have everything he wanted? Wasn't he happy? Didn't he go to church and live according to the rules? So he started to look for something to blame. He comes to the conclusion that there was something outside himself that caused his trouble. He didn't do anything to cause it. Certainly not. But let's analyze his case, and what do we find. He was getting along fine. He wasn't short in anything. He made one little mistake. He allowed himself to become overconfident. Instead of thanking God for his good fortune and choosing to keep it that way, he chose to become careless and . . . not realizing, deliberately choosing to do something to GET BACK INTO TROUBLE AGAIN. This overconfidence has done as much to spoil and frequently to ruin as many lives as any other reason we might know of. Very little is ever said about overconfidence. We are not aware of it. It over-takes us because we have failed to recognize this GREATEST POWER . . . THE POWER TO CHOOSE . . . with the result that we are not careful at a time when we should be. Nature does not want us underconfident . . . but she does not want us to be overconfident. Millions of people have had a taste of overconfidence . . . without recognizing it. If they don't recognize it, they may be kicked down by it, and may never get up again. Then when it happens, it takes the spirit out of their lives. They are defeated and beaten. They cannot analyze what happened, with the result that another life joins the great ranks of discouraged people.

George gets a raise in salary. He comes home as happy as can be. He says to his wife, "Let's go out and celebrate." They call up another couple and go to some night club to celebrate. They start to drink. Before long George is making love to the other man's wife. His wife is now making love to the husband of the other couple. Now George doesn't like it. They start to argue. They come home in a rage. The argument continues into the early hours of the morning. After it is all over, George wishes he had never gotten the raise. Then, he sits down and begins to complain. He complains that his happiness did not last long, that his good luck was short-lived. But why? Because something outside himself brought it about? Because God did not want him to be happy? Why? You know why . . . now. George's good fortune made him overconfident. His overconfidence led to carelessness . . . carelessness almost always leads to trouble.

Most people cannot stand life when it runs along "TOO SMOOTHLY." They crave excitement. They crave it because they choose it. This choice brings them into a troubled state and then they say "THIS IS LIFE." Life did not produce the trouble. We bring it about ourselves with our BAD CHOICE OF THOUGHT.

From time to time we hear people say, "If I can put this deal across, then I don't care what happens." "If I marry George, then I don't care what happens." "After we get the mortgage paid, then I don't care what happens." WHAT A TERRIBLE CHOICE OF THOUGHT! How stupid! Can you see why there is so much trouble in the world, and why so few people are really happy? Imagine choosing the thought . . . "I don't care what happens." It is almost like going into a restaurant and saying, "I don't care what you serve me as long as it is food." They may serve you food that is so badly burned that you can't even eat it. They may serve you meat that you can't even cut. They may serve a vegetable that is so badly rotted that you can't even look at it. BE CAREFUL. It is just as easy to be careful, as it is to be careless. YOU DO CARE WHAT HAPPENS AND YOU KNOW IT. Keep thinking good thoughts. Keep thoughts that will help you, not harm you. It is important, because through this GREATEST POWER . . . THE POWER TO CHOOSE . . . LIFE BECOMES WHAT YOU THINK AND CHOOSE IT TO BE.

Our parents, our grandparents, our great-grandparents and people for generations back have so completely filled our minds with the thought that we must have trouble; that this, that, and the other is too good to last; that we of this modern day and age have come to inherit these thoughts which *keep the world in mental bondage.*

THE POWER TO CHOOSE gave the young man in our story a NEW FREEDOM. He slept better. He felt better. He realized that there was nothing outside himself trying to hurt him or destroy his happiness. He began to live. HE FOUND A NEW LEASE ON LIFE. He began to realize that there *WASN'T SOMETHING* THAT ALWAYS HAPPENS TO SPOIL HIS LIFE. *THAT SOME-*

THING was his own failure TO CHOOSE CORRECTLY. Once he realized this simple, yet POWERFUL FORCE, his whole life changed. He knew that IT WAS HIS OWN THOUGHTS . . . HIS OWN CHOOSING that caused his trouble and not some unseen force or power outside himself. (Read this last statement again and again.)

All over the world people CHOOSE TO BELIEVE that if it isn't one thing, it's another. People everywhere are bewildered by the thought . . . if it isn't one thing, it's another. A man is working steadily . . . everything is moving along without friction . . . EVERYTHING EXCEPT HIS OWN THINKING. He starts his mind into action. He says, "Yes, I am working now, but how long will it last?" Before long, he is out of work. The grocery bill begins to mount; the back rent becomes a worry; work is not in sight; his child takes sick; then he takes sick. A big doctor bill faces him, together with all the other expenses of the household. The man has to go to the hospital. The hospital bill makes life even more uncomfortable. Finally, the man goes back to work. He begins to pay up his debts. He is just about straightened out and paid up on all his bills when something else appears . . . and so . . . with a few experiences of this kind he becomes a

CONFIRMED BELIEVER in the thought . . . THAT IF IT ISN'T ONE THING, IT'S ANOTHER.

During all this trouble period, he found himself carried away with his trouble and his trouble thoughts. He never did think clearly, mainly because he was never taught to think clearly, and he just never did learn to think clearly on his own. He had his "ACRES OF DIAMONDS," but he never found them. He remained poor in his thoughts, and poor thoughts bring poor results. Had he discovered his GREATEST POWER . . . THE POWER TO CHOOSE . . . he would then have realized that most of his trouble was due to his own poor thinking. THEN IF HE HAD DISCOVERED THAT NOTHING IS TOO GOOD TO LAST, he could have avoided his difficulties and instead of expecting trouble, he would have expected his smooth-running life to continue.

It isn't easy to live an even-going life, when we notice that everyone around us is filled with trouble, difficulties and disappointments. However, when we begin to realize that those who are filled with troubles and difficulties are using their GREATEST POWER . . . THE POWER TO CHOOSE . . . AND USING IT INCORRECTLY, then we begin to understand why things happen the way they do. Is it any wonder that so many people "knock on wood" when things are going along nicely. The fear THAT IT IS TOO GOOD TO LAST is obvious and apparent. We must constantly remind ourselves . . . THAT NOTHING IS TOO GOOD TO LAST . . . and before long we will begin to believe it. When enough of us begin to believe it and practice it . . . we will . . . just as Columbus discovered a new world in 1492 . . . DISCOVER A NEW WORLD OF REAL LIVING.

One of the greatest of religious leaders, head of one of the large Eastern religions, said, "How can I be happy, when the rest of the world is unhappy?" A very good question, and being a very wise man he presented a very interesting problem. However, if we see no man happy then we come to the conclusion that life is not meant to be happy. When we are happy for a short time, we must of necessity come to the conclusion that it is not meant to last. But, why not? If this great religious leader had said instead, "Look at me . . . look how happy I am . . . you can be the same as I . . . if you will follow my teachings." Then his millions of followers would have felt that it is natural to be happy, and at least one of the great religions of the world would have had millions of happy people. Again, we see that one man can change an entire group of people, running into the millions. Like many of our new inventions, no one thought of them before. Likewise, before Florence Shinn came out with the statement NOTHING IS TOO GOOD TO LAST . . . people thought that happiness could not last . . . because so few people had been able to demonstrate it. This great religious leader has THE POWER TO CHOOSE. He chose to believe that he could not be happy because the rest of the world was not. What was to stop him from choosing to set an example of happiness for his followers? Nothing, but his OWN CHOICE.

The same conditions that prevail with an individual can also prevail with a whole country. So many people remember when everything in the nation was going along smoothly. Almost everybody was working, there was very little unemployment. People were buying new cars; stocks were high; property was high; everybody seemed to be making money. Most people seemed to be riding on the crest of the waves. For a short period of time it seemed as though the world was having one of the greatest periods of prosperity that it had ever seen. But many people from the richest to the poorest, from the weakest to the strongest, from the lowest to the highest walks of life, began to feel that IT WAS TOO GOOD TO LAST. Little by little this thought began to fill the minds of the people everywhere. Things began to change. People became cautious. Stocks began to topple. Banks began to close. Everywhere there was nothing but darkness and despair. A land that yesterday was prosperous, was now thrown into the depths of depression, all because from the richest to the poorest, people felt that IT WAS TOO GOOD TO LAST.

What would have happened if these same millions of people who said it was too good to last would have used their GREATEST POWER and had CHOSEN TO BELIEVE THAT NOTHING IS TOO GOOD TO LAST? THEY WOULD HAVE FOUND A WAY TO KEEP THINGS RUNNING ALONG SMOOTHLY. As one man said, "This is truly a great country." When the country seemed to be at a standstill and was not going forward, the automobile came along and kept everybody busy and progressive. When we seemed to catch up with ourselves with the automobile and it seemed that everything would be at a standstill, the airplane began to pick up the slack in our production. Then when the airplane seemed to fill its need, the radio began to take up the slack . . . after radio came television. THIS ONE

MAN CHOSE TO BELIEVE THAT NOTHING IS
TOO GOOD TO LAST. *SOMETHING GOOD
CAN HAPPEN* . . . just as easily as something bad.
WE MUST USE THIS POWER TO CHOOSE
CORRECTLY OR IT WILL WORK THE VERY
OPPOSITE OF THE WAY WE WOULD LIKE LIFE
TO BE.

There are still millions upon millions of people
in this world who have nothing. There are still
millions upon millions of people on this earth who
do not have a single change of clothing. Millions are
not properly housed. The world as a whole is still
unlearned and uneducated. According to the reports,
two-thirds of the world still eat without knives and
forks. Even in this country, there are still millions of
people without bathtubs, without decent living quar-
ters, without hope of ever seeing a better way of life.

LET US CHOOSE TO BELIEVE
THAT SOMETHING GOOD CAN HAPPEN.
WHY MUST WE ALWAYS USE
THE OLD MODEL . . . THAT
SOMETHING BAD WILL HAPPEN?

We begin to realize now that through the
GREATEST POWER . . . THE POWER TO

CHOOSE . . . that man has come a long way since the first man walked the face of the earth. The world, as a result of modern inventions is reaching a point that it is gradually mastering the forces of nature, in as far as the mechanical perfections that go to make life more enjoyable are endless. With this mastering of nature, we begin to realize now that we have a bigger job . . . MASTERING OURSELVES. We have gone through the stone age, the wood age, the iron age, just going through the mechanical age . . . we are now entering the MENTAL AGE. Man has been using . . . those who have used it . . . THE POWER TO CHOOSE and not realizing it. Now that we realize it . . . we make the great discovery that most of our troubles, our difficulties, and our miseries are *MAN MADE.*

Man has been making himself a mechanical life of ease and pleasure; while at the same time he has been making his mental life more and more complicated. It need not be; not any more. NOW THAT HE HAS DISCOVERED THIS GREATEST POWER . . . THE POWER TO CHOOSE . . . HE CAN CHOOSE TO LIVE . . . LIKE A MAN.

No longer can man blame something outside of himself. Man must blame himself. Man does what he does because . . . HE CHOOSES THUS TO DO.

Maybe we won't admit it, but it is true. For years man worked the whole day through, sometimes putting in 12 to 14 hours a day, with little or no time for leisure. As a result of modern inventions, man has more time for himself. Man, therefore, is at the present time, beginning to fathom the art of real living. He must learn how to live because he has so much leisure time on his hands. As long as he has so much time on his hands, he must be able to use it sensibly. If he doesn't, he will bring destruction upon himself. Man has found that tasks that were difficult years ago, are now simplified by machinery. Man will now find time to learn how to live. In learning how to live, he will recognize that the most important task is TO LEARN HOW TO LIVE WITH HIMSELF. He will learn to live with himself when he begins to use THE GREATEST POWER THAT HE POSSESSES . . . THE POWER TO CHOOSE.

This GREATEST POWER . . . THE POWER TO CHOOSE . . . will make life for him what he always wanted it to be; not to depend upon something outside of himself, but to depend on that great POWER WITHIN HIMSELF, THIS GOD-GIVEN POWER WHICH MAKES HIM A MAN. He will realize that life does not depend on money, machines, cars, homes, furs, and so-called wealth . . . but upon his MIND POWER given to him by the UNIVERSAL MIND POWER of which he is a part, and through which all that he desires can come to pass.

Man must realize that the most important thing in life is LIFE. Therefore, he owes his first duty to this LIFE which he possesses. If he takes care of his LIFE, it will be what he wants it to be. If he neglects his own LIFE . . . it will be what he does not want it to be. After the UNIVERSAL POWER gives man LIFE . . . then it is up to MAN TO CHOOSE TO DO WITH IT AS HE SEES FIT.

May we remind you of a poem we came across some time ago:

> "I shall pass through this world but once
> Any good, therefore, that I can do,
> Or any kindness that I can show
> To any human being,
> Let me do it now. Let me
> Not defer it or neglect it,
> For I shall not pass this way again."

Therefore, the fact remains that inasmuch as we are going through life JUST ONCE, we should choose to make life a confident one, instead of a timid one . . . that we should choose to make a calm life rather than one of restlessness . . . that we should choose to have poise rather than confusion . . . that we should choose to make the most of life for ourselves and everyone else around us . . . rather than spoil our own lives and those about us. We have the POWER TO CHOOSE . . . LET US USE IT TO THE BEST OF OUR ABILITY. As we use our own minds to CHOOSE THE BEST so we will find that the UNIVERSAL MIND will come to our aid and assistance to help us choose the BEST. Together we cannot fail. WE MUST SUCCEED!

JUST AN AFTERTHOUGHT

Now that you have read "YOUR GREATEST POWER," do you feel better? Sure you do. Then read it over and over again.

Anytime you find yourself a little disgusted, disturbed, or upset, read it. You'll feel better.

Keep a copy at your bedside. Read a little before you go to sleep. You will feel better and stronger the next morning.

Why not send a copy to someone who needs it? It will be appreciated, to be sure.

HIDDEN TREASURE

It exists in self-help books such as *Your Greatest Power.* Here's how to find it.

By W. Clement Stone

Let's try an experiment: When you see a word, phrase or sentence that is underscored in this article, just copy the number beside it and write down the thoughts, if any, that flash in your mind. Try it! Something wonderful may happen to you if you subsequently relate the idea, suggestion or principle to yourself. I'll explain why the experiment later.

Everyone loves an adventure story! Countless readers have been intrigued with tales of: pioneers and cowboys who opened the American West . . .

Flash Gordon and Buck Rogers keeping Planet Earth safe from evil forces of outer space . . . brave explorers going into deep jungles filled with danger to find ruins of past civilizations . . . swashbuckling seamen fighting off the attacks of pirates . . . and stories of: *TREASURE* . . . hidden treasure—lost gold mines and—sunken treasure ships. These are among the stories that have caused so many of us to daydream. Perhaps each of us, at least once, has fantasized finding a map that would lead us to our particular fanciful *TREASURE*. The word itself conjures up visions of chests laden with gold, silver, jewels beyond price.

Stories of great adventure appeared in the news media recently that may trigger such a dream and stimulate our imaginations to help us materialize maps whereby we shall find hidden treasures. But this applies only to those of us who have learned HOW TO develop the habit of taking ACTION when we recognize a usable principle and relate it to ourselves from what we read, hear, see, think or experience.

TREASURE BENEATH THE SEA

While reading the *Chicago Tribune* of Sunday,

January 21, 1979, a headline caught my eye: "Drama, Treasure Beneath the Sea." Written by Carol Oppenheim, a *Tribune* writer and certified scuba diver who went into the sea with the treasure hunters, the article related the story of the discovery of the Spanish galleon *Concepcion*. As I had learned at an early age HOW TO Recognize, Relate, Assimilate, and Apply principles, it flashed into my mind that the concepts in Carol's account would be an excellent basis for this article. The following is a summary of Carol's article:

The *Concepcion* sailed from Mexico in 1641, heavily loaded with silver coins, gold ingots, Chinese porcelain and countless tons of other booty claimed by the Spanish crown. Not listed on the manifest were contraband smuggled aboard by the officers and crew, which may have accounted for 20 to 50 percent of the cargo.

A few weeks out of Vera Cruz, the *Concepcion* ran into an eight-day storm. With her masts gone, she limped toward Puerto Rico to make repairs. Eighty miles off Hispaniola, now the Dominican Republic, the ship rammed into the coral reefs and foundered.

In 1687, William Phips found the wreck and, employing native divers who could stay underwater only three minutes at a time, recovered 32 tons of silver.

Burt Webber, 36, who grew up in central Pennsylvania, developed a "fascination with water" when he was 6 years old. When interviewed, he said, "We had a mountain stream running into a mill, and I would swim in it, fantasizing about being on the bottom instead of the top . . . I began reading books on shipwrecks, and I knew I wanted to dive."[1] At 16, Webber sold his coin collection to buy a scuba tank.[2]

Webber "wanted to join the Navy but could not pass the physical because of his asthma. Instead, he enrolled in the Divers Training Academy in Miami."[3] In 1961, he "was hired by the Museum of Sunken Treasure in the Florida Keys." He took part in many treasure hunts,[4] some of which "met expenses."[5]

Five years ago, Webber decided to "shoot for a big one."[6] He and Jack Haskins, 44, another treasure hunter based in Florida, were competitors until they decided to join forces[7] a decade ago. Haskins became Webber's researcher,[8] making annual trips to Spain to study naval archives. In 1974, Haskins came across documents[9] detailing the aborted voyage of the Concepcion. He deduced that Phips hadn't picked the wreck clean[10] . . . what remained would be very lucrative, easy to find and easy to salvage since the shoals bottomed at an average depth of 65 feet.

Armed with this information . . . a consortium of 30 investors[11] raised $450,000 and set up a corporation now known as Sequest International to negotiate a contract with the Dominican Republic[12] providing for a 50-50 split of the treasure.

Equipped with a magnetometer[13] to record anomalies in the coral, Webber and Haskins, accompanied by a crew of divers, American map and coin experts[14] and a Dominican naval officer, searched the reef for five months in 1977. They found 13 wrecks . . . none the Concepcion. "I bet we went right over her,"[15] Haskins said later, "but our mag' wasn't sensitive enough to catch it."

A year later, the treasure hunters learned that the log of Henry Phips's ship had been found. It contained the precise compass points for the location of the lost galleon.[16] In mid-November, carrying a newly developed portable magnetometer, the group set out again aboard the *Samala*. On the sixth day of the renewed search, the divers found an iron strap and a 17th century Spanish olive jar. Three days later—November 30—they found the first silver coin.[17]

"Then we just kept pulling up coins—130 that first day . . . " plus cups, plates, candlesticks, candle snuffers and more olive jars. They found so much they decided that numismatist Henry Taylor would have to move his operations to shore. Taylor chipped away the shards of coral and bathed the coins in muriatic acid. What he saw were rough-shaped circles containing about one ounce of silver, bearing the cross and shield of the king of Spain and the dates 1630 through 1640— proof, he and other experts said, the coins were from the *Concepcion*.

" . . . The crew twice has discovered a complete chest of coins fused by the coral into a solid 180-pound mass."

Webber refused to discuss the potential

value of the booty. Published reports place it at $40 million, but there is speculation it might be as much as five times greater. The salvage operation is expected to continue for months, interrupted only by trips to Santo Domingo to unload the treasure and take on food and water. Haskins believes the section of reef now being worked was not the location of the *Concepcion's* main hold . . . and may not even have been touched by Phips's divers.

Important Points in Discovering Hidden Treasures

I have had many investment opportunities submitted to me . . . among them, to become one of Burt Webber's investors in the search for the *Concepcion*. However, because I had treasure maps of my own, I decided against joining the consortium. On my maps, "X" marks the spot (the goal) where there are riches . . . and many of them are treasures money can't buy. I am now sharing with you several of the important points necessary in reading or interpreting any map that leads to the discovery of hidden treasures.

Do you want to find a hidden treasure? Now

you can. But, like Burt Webber and Jack Haskins, you must carefully study, understand and comprehend why it is imperative to follow directions to achieve your objectives. It may be tough to get started, but it will become easier and easier as you get experience in developing the necessary habits of thought and action as you travel toward your destination.

So Obvious It Isn't Seen

Long ago, I developed the habit of underscoring words, phrases and entire sentences while reading a newspaper, magazine, book or other printed material for the purpose of recognizing key ideas that symbolize principles such as those employed by Burt Webber and Jack Haskins that made their dreams become a reality . . . principles so obvious that they may not be seen unless you establish the habit of Recognizing, Relating, Assimilating and then APPLYING those which can bring you to where "X" marks the spot on the map.

The interpretation of the underscoring above can be a guideline in helping you to develop an accurate map to find any treasure you may choose to seek. But you must first know specifically what you want and develop an intense desire to get it. That is what Burt and Jack did. That is the one thing that separates the achievers from the dreamers.

As you read on, I shall describe the principles I recognized. This may help you to design your treasure map. Let's compare notes: If you followed the instructions in the introduction to this article, you will want to refer back to the numbers and compare your notes with mine as to what each idea you selected symbolized or represented.

17 PRINCIPLES

1. A desire that motivated Burt to set a definite goal: to dive.

2. Paying the price and . . . Budgeting time and money.

3. Learning from defeat . . . "With every adversity, there is a seed of an equivalent or greater benefit for those who have PMA (a Positive Mental Attitude)."

4. Gaining experience in seeking a treasure.

5. Again, learning from defeat . . . The value of perseverance.

6. Aiming high . . . Definiteness of purpose.

7. The Master Mind Alliance.

8. Accurate thinking . . . Teamwork.

9. Controlled attention. With a definite goal, one is apt to recognize that which will help him achieve it, particularly if he develops a burning desire.

10. Thinking . . . Planning and . . . Study time.

11. Use of Other People's Money (OPM).

12. Good legal advice to get the cooperation of the government and prevent confiscation of the treasure.

13. Use of modern equipment.

14. The employment of experts.

15. PMA . . . Learning from defeat . . . Accurate thinking (to get better equipment).

16. "Success is achieved by those who try and maintained by those who keep trying with PMA."

17. "What the mind of man can conceive and

believe, the mind of man can achieve for those who have PMA."

The list includes many of the principles to be found in Napoleon Hill's *Law of Success, Think and Grow Rich* and *Success Through a Positive Mental Attitude,* coauthored by Dr. Hill and me. In addition, you may wish to reexamine the story "Drama, Treasure Beneath the Sea" to determine whether other principles, not mentioned, are applicable such as: Going the extra mile . . . Self-discipline . . . Applied faith . . . Pleasing personality . . . Personal initiative . . . Enthusiasm . . . Creative vision . . . Maintaining sound physical and mental health . . . Using cosmic habit force (universal law).

DO YOU WANT TO FIND A HIDDEN TREASURE? . . . HERE'S HOW!

Do you want to find a hidden treasure. I have my treasure maps. Now you can have yours. Just use your mind power as Burt Webber, Jack Haskins and everyone else has who found treasures—tangible or intangible—including the true riches of life. They Recognized, Related, Assimilated and APPLIED the PMA principles revealed to you in this article.

72

The map is now in your hands. *Will you dream of achievements . . . or achieve your dreams?*

For additional information about Napoleon Hill products, please contact the following locations:

The Napoleon Hill World Learning Center
Purdue University Calumet
2300 173rd Street
Hammond, IN 46323-2094

Judith Williamson, Director
Uriel "Chino" Martinez, Assistant/Graphic Designer

Telephone: 219-989-3173 or 219-989-3166
email: nhf@calumet.purdue.edu

The Napoleon Hill Foundation
University of Virginia-Wise
College Relations Apt. C
1 College Avenue
Wise, VA 24293

Don Green, Executive Director
Annedia Sturgill, Executive Assistant

Telephone: 276-328-6700
email: napoleonhill@uvawise.edu

Website: www.naphill.org